PIANO • VOCAL • GUITAR

more of THE BEST JAZZ STANDARDS EVER

Date: 1/19/12

ISBN 0-634-06331-6

HAL•LEONARD®
CORPORATION
7777 W. BLUEMOUND RD. P.O. BOX 13819 MILWAUKEE, WI 53213

Visit Hal Leonard Online at
www.halleonard.com

more of THE BEST JAZZ STANDARDS EVER

CONTENTS

4   Água de beber (Water to Drink)
8   Ain't Misbehavin'
13   All or Nothing at All
20   Alright, Okay, You Win
25   Angel Eyes
28   Autumn Leaves
38   Blue in Green
40   Blue Skies
31   Bluesette
44   Cast Your Fate to the Wind
48   Cheek to Cheek
53   Cherokee (Indian Love Song)
58   The Coffee Song (They've Got an Awful Lot of Coffee in Brazil)
62   Come Fly with Me
68   Come Rain or Come Shine
74   Cotton Tail
71   Could It Be You
76   Darn That Dream
84   Dedicated to You
79   Devil May Care
88   Dreamy
92   East of the Sun (And West of the Moon)
95   Easy Living
98   Easy to Love (You'd Be So Easy to Love)
101   Feels So Good
106   Fly Me to the Moon (In Other Words)
112   The Frim Fram Sauce
116   The Girl from Ipanema (Garôta de Ipanema)
109   Girl Talk
120   Harlem Nocturne
125   Haven't We Met
130   Honeysuckle Rose
133   How Deep Is the Ocean (How High Is the Sky)
136   How High the Moon
142   How Insensitive (Insensatez)

146 I Remember You

150 I Thought About You

139 I'm Beginning to See the Light

154 I've Got the World on a String

162 I've Grown Accustomed to Her Face

159 In a Mellow Tone

164 In Walked Bud

170 It Never Entered My Mind

174 The Lady Is a Tramp

167 The Look of Love

178 Love Letters

182 Lullaby of Birdland

186 Meditation (Meditacáo)

189 Moon River

192 My Favorite Things

196 My Foolish Heart

199 My Funny Valentine

204 My One and Only Love

207 A Nightingale Sang in Berkeley Square

212 Nuages

214 Oh! Look at Me Now

217 Old Devil Moon

220 Rio De Janeiro Blue

228 Ruby, My Dear

225 Sentimental Journey

230 Speak Low

235 Stardust

240 Stompin' at the Savoy

243 Street Life

250 Suddenly It's Spring

254 So Nice (Summer Samba)

257 Tenderly

260 There Will Never Be Another You

263 There's a Small Hotel

266 Watch What Happens

269 What a Diff'rence a Day Made

272 When I Fall in Love

274 Where or When

278 Willow Weep for Me

ÁGUA DE BEBER
(Water to Drink)

English Words by NORMAN GIMBEL
Portuguese Words by VINICIUS DE MORAES
Music by ANTONIO CARLOS JOBIM

Your love ___ is rain, ___

my heart ___ the flow - er. ___
on dis - tant de - serts. ___

Portuguese Lyrics

Eu quis amar Mas tive medo
E quis salvar meu corração
Mas o amor sabe um segredo
O medo pode matar o seu coração

Água de beber
Água de beber camará
Água de beber
Água de beber camará

Eu nunca fiz coisa tão certa
Entrei pra escola do perdão
A minha casa vive aberta
Abre todas as portas do coração

Água de beber...

Eu sempre tive uma certeza
Que só me deu desilusão
É que o amor É uma tristeza
Muita mágoa demais para um coração

Água de beber...

AIN'T MISBEHAVIN'
from AIN'T MISBEHAVIN'

Words by ANDY RAZAF
Music by THOMAS "FATS" WALLER
and HARRY BROOKS

ALL OR NOTHING AT ALL

Words by JACK LAWRENCE
Music by ARTHUR ALTMAN

ALRIGHT, OKAY, YOU WIN

Words and Music by SID WYCHE
and MAYME WATTS

Moderately, with rhythm

ANGEL EYES

Words by EARL BRENT
Music by MATT DENNIS

AUTUMN LEAVES

English lyric by JOHNNY MERCER
French lyric by JACQUES PREVERT
Music by JOSEPH KOSMA

Oh! je vou-drais tant que tu te sou-viennes, des jours heu-reux où nous é-tions a - mis.
Les Feuil-les Mortes se ra-massent à la pelle, les sou-ve-nirs et les re-grets aus-si.

En ce temps-là la vie é-tait plus belle et le so-leil plus brû-lant qu'au-jourd-'hui.
Mais mon a-mour si-len-cieux et fi-dèle sou-rit tou-jours et re-mer-cie la vie.

Les Feuil-les Mortes se ra-massent à la pelle, Tu vois, je n'ai pas ou-bli-é.
Je t'ai-mais tant, tu é-tais si jo-lie, Com-ment veux-tu que je t'ou-blie.

BLUESETTE

Words by NORMAN GIMBEL
Music by JEAN THIELEMANS

Moderate Waltz

Poor lit-tle, sad lit-tle blue Blues-ette.
Long as there's sad love in your blue heart to share,

Don't you cry, don't you fret.
dear Blues-ette, don't de - spair.

BLUE IN GREEN

By MILES DAVIS

Slowly

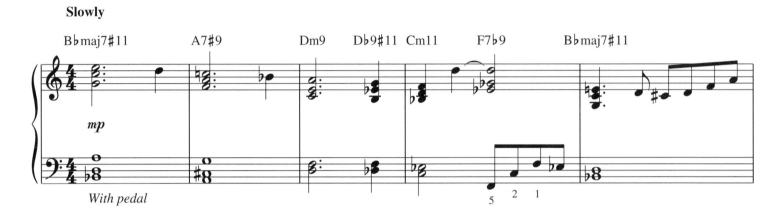

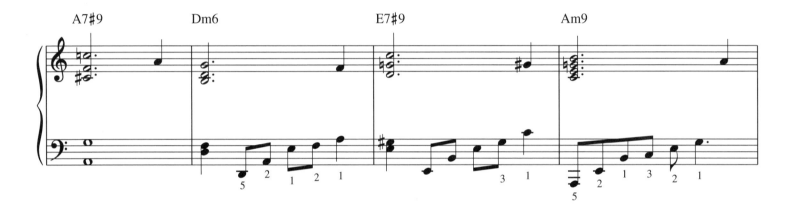

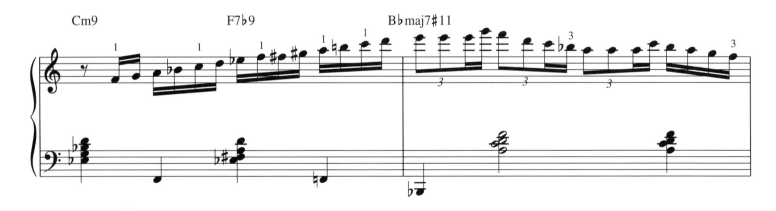

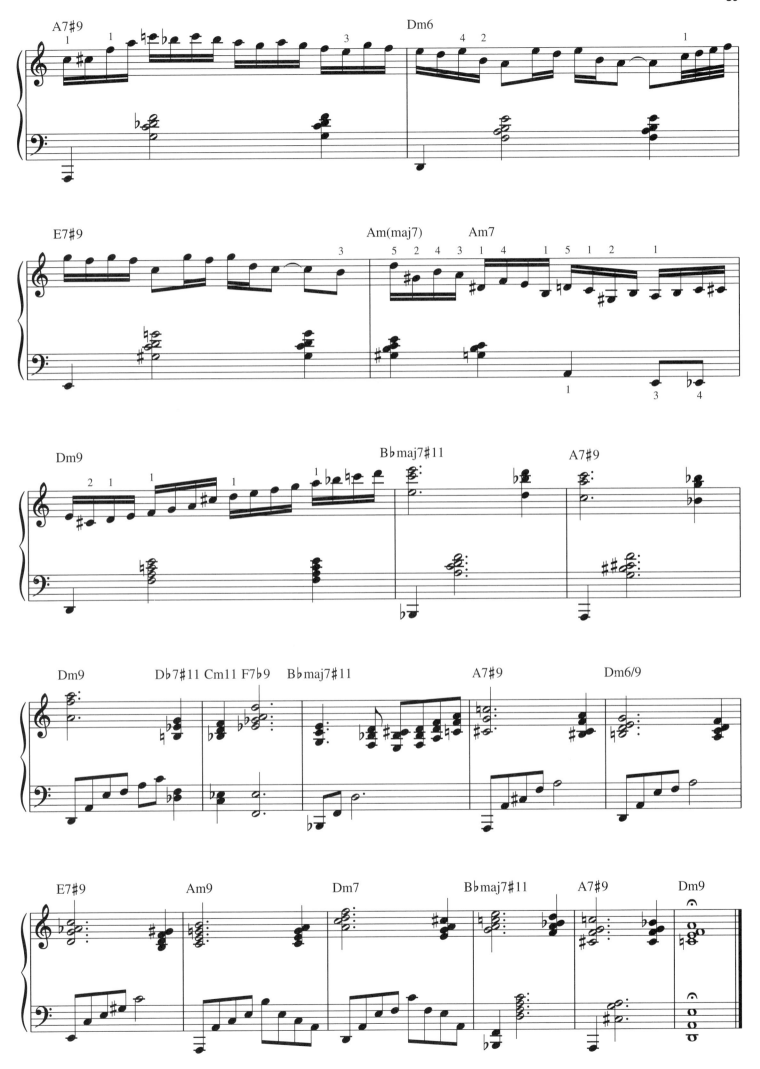

BLUE SKIES

from BETSY

Words and Music by
IRVING BERLIN

CAST YOUR FATE TO THE WIND

Words and Music by VINCE GUARALDI
and CAREL WERVER

CHEEK TO CHEEK
from the RKO Radio Motion Picture TOP HAT

Words and Music by
IRVING BERLIN

CHEROKEE
(Indian Love Song)

Words and Music by
RAY NOBLE

THE COFFEE SONG
(They've Got an Awful Lot of Coffee in Brazil)

Words and Music by BOB HILLIARD
and DICK MILES

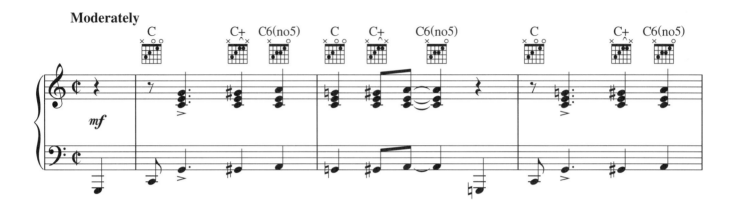

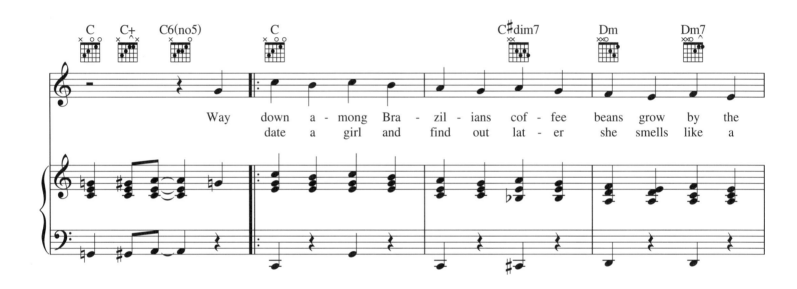

Way down a-mong Bra-zil-ians cof-fee beans grow by the
date a girl and find out lat-er she smells like a

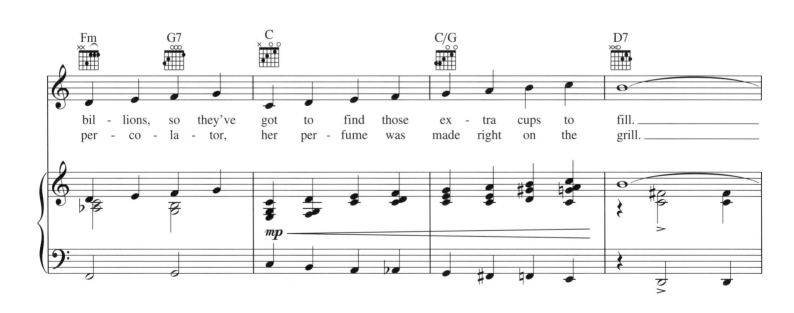

bil - lions, so they've got to find those ex - tra cups to fill. ___
per - co - la - tor, her per - fume was made right on the grill. ___

COME FLY WITH ME

Words by SAMMY CAHN
Music by JAMES VAN HEUSEN

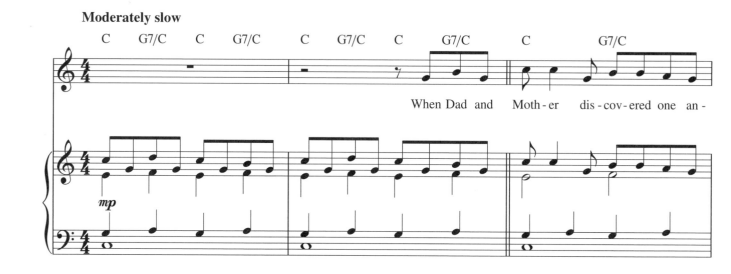

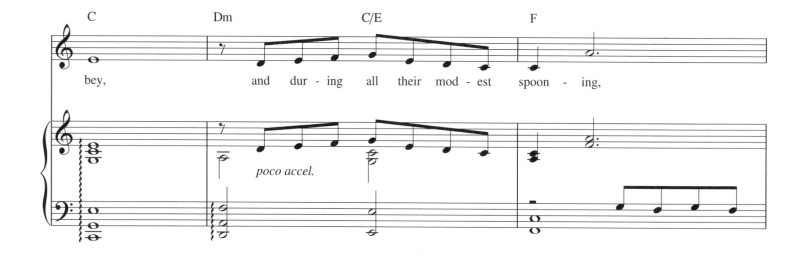

COME RAIN OR COME SHINE

from ST. LOUIS WOMAN

Words by JOHNNY MERCER
Music by HAROLD ARLEN

COULD IT BE YOU

Words and Music by
COLE PORTER

Lyrics:

A white sea-shore in moon-light im-mersed, A si-lent palm-tree sway-ing,

When out of no-where you sud-den-ly burst, And I found my-self say-ing:

Could it be you, The one I'm fat-ed for? __

COTTON TAIL

By DUKE ELLINGTON

DARN THAT DREAM

Lyric by EDDIE DE LANGE
Music by JIMMY VAN HEUSEN

Darn that dream I
Darn your dream lips and

dream each night, you say you love me and you
darn your eyes, they lift me high above the

hold me tight, but when I a- wake you're
moon- lit skies, then I tum- ble out of

DEVIL MAY CARE

Words and Music by BOB DOROUGH
and TERRELL P. KIRK, JR.

Original key: Bb minor. *This edition has been transposed up one whole step to be more playable.*

DEDICATED TO YOU

Words and Music by SAMMY CAHN,
SAUL CHAPLIN and HY ZARET

DREAMY

Music by ERROLL GARNER
Lyric by SYDNEY SHAW

Ballad tempo

Ask me why I have this smile up-on my face,_ Ask me

why I see a rain-bow out in space,_ Well, I

must con-fess,_____ you don't need a ge-nius to guess

EAST OF THE SUN
(And West of the Moon)

Words and Music by
BROOKS BOWMAN

EASY LIVING

Theme from the Paramount Picture EASY LIVING

Words and Music by LEO ROBIN
and RALPH RAINGER

EASY TO LOVE
(You'd Be So Easy to Love)
from BORN TO DANCE

Words and Music by
COLE PORTER

Moderately

You'd be so eas-y to love, so eas-y to i-dol-ize, all oth-ers a-bove, so

FEELS SO GOOD

In a bright 2

Words and Music by
CHUCK MANGIONE

FLY ME TO THE MOON
(In Other Words)
featured in the Motion Picture ONCE AROUND

Words and Music by
BART HOWARD

Bossa Nova

Fly me to the moon, ___ and let me play a - mong the stars; ___

Let me see what spring ___ is like on

Ju - pi - ter and Mars. ___ In oth - er words, ___

GIRL TALK
from the Paramount Picture HARLOW

Words by BOBBY TROUP
Music by NEAL HEFTI

THE FRIM FRAM SAUCE

Words and Music by JOE RICARDEL
and REDD EVANS

THE GIRL FROM IPANEMA
(Garôta de Ipanema)

Music by ANTONIO CARLOS JOBIM
English Words by NORMAN GIMBEL
Original Words by VINICIUS DE MORAES

HARLEM NOCTURNE

Words by DICK ROGERS
Music by EARLE HAGEN

HAVEN'T WE MET

Words and Music by RUTH BATCHELOR
and KENNY RANKIN

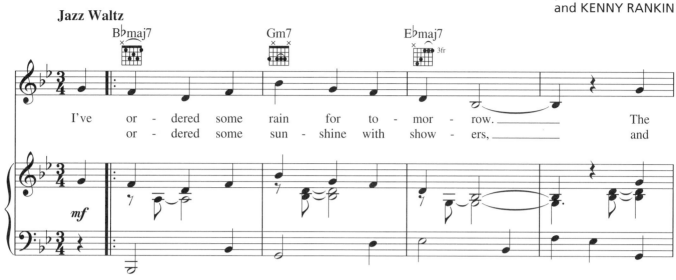

I've or-dered some rain for to-mor-row. _____ The
or-dered some sun-shine with show-ers, _____ and

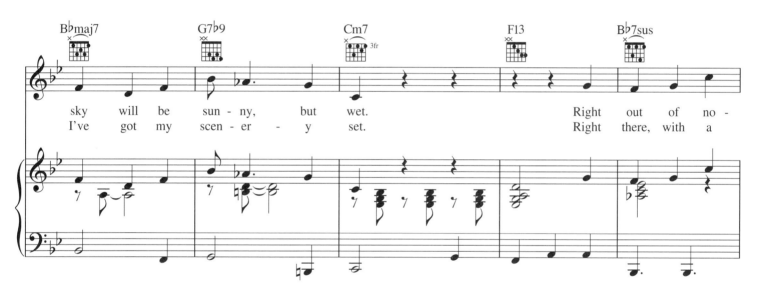

sky will be sun-ny, but wet. Right out of no a-
I've got my scen-er-y set. Right there, with a

where, you're sud-den-ly there, and I say "Par - don
thump, our um-brel-las will bump, and I'll say "Par - don

HONEYSUCKLE ROSE

from AIN'T MISBEHAVIN'
from TIN PAN ALLEY

Words by ANDY RAZAF
Music by THOMAS "FATS" WALLER

HOW DEEP IS THE OCEAN
(How High Is the Sky)

Words and Music by
IRVING BERLIN

HOW HIGH THE MOON

from TWO FOR THE SHOW

Words by NANCY HAMILTON
Music by MORGAN LEWIS

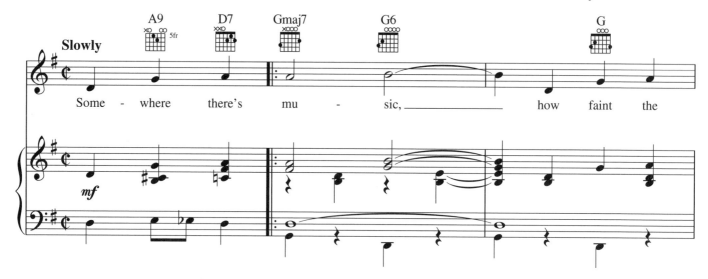

Slowly

Some - where there's mu - sic, _____ how faint the

tune! _____ Some - where there's heav - en, _____

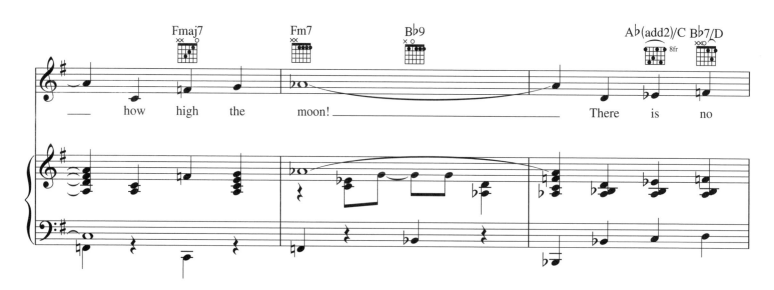

___ how high the moon! There is no

I'M BEGINNING TO SEE THE LIGHT

Words and Music by DON GEORGE, JOHNNY HODGES,
DUKE ELLINGTON and HARRY JAMES

8vb

HOW INSENSITIVE
(Insensatez)

Music by ANTONIO CARLOS JOBIM
Original Words by VINICIUS DE MORAES
English Words by NORMAN GIMBEL

Lyrics:

How _____ in-sen-si-tive _____
Now, _____ {he's / she's} gone a-way _____

_____ I must have seemed _____ when he told me that {he / she} loved _____ me. _____
_____ and I'm _____ a-lone _____ with the mem-'ry of _____ {his / her} last _____ look. _____

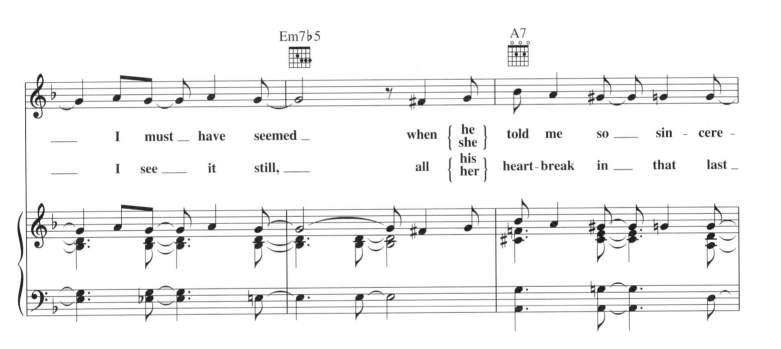

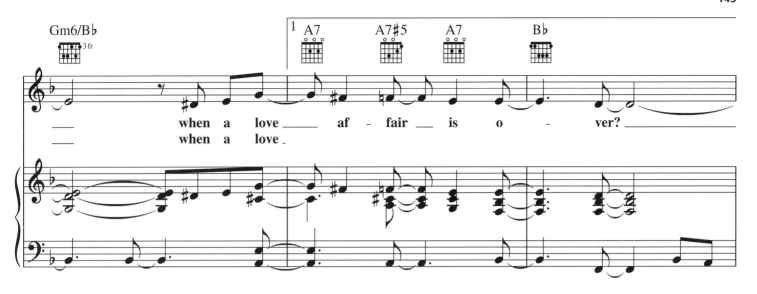

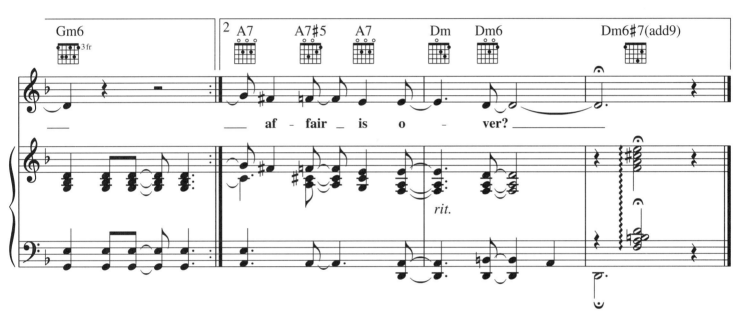

Portuguese Lyrics

A insensatez
Que você fez
Coração mais sem cuidado
Fez chorar de dôr
O seu amôr
Um amôr tão delicado
Ah! Porque você
Foi fraco assim
Assim tão desalmado
Ah! Meu coração
Que nunca amou
Não merece ser amado
Vai meu coração
Ouve a razão
Usa só sinceridade
Quem semeia vento
Diz a razão
Colhe tempestade
Vai meu coração
Pede perdão
Perdão apaixonado
Vai porque
Quem não
Pede perdão
Não é nunca perdoado.

I REMEMBER YOU

from the Paramount Picture THE FLEET'S IN

Words by JOHNNY MERCER
Music by VICTOR SCHERTZINGER

I THOUGHT ABOUT YOU

Words by JOHNNY MERCER
Music by JIMMY VAN HEUSEN

I'VE GOT THE WORLD ON A STRING

Lyric by TED KOEHLER
Music by HAROLD ARLEN

Mer - ry month of May, sun - ny

IN A MELLOW TONE

Words by MILT GABLER
Music by DUKE ELLINGTON

I'VE GROWN ACCUSTOMED TO HER FACE

from MY FAIR LADY

Words by ALAN JAY LERNER
Music by FREDERICK LOEWE

I've grown ac-cus-tomed to her face; _____ she al-most
cus-tomed to her face; _____ she al-most

makes the day be-gin. _____ I've grown ac-cus-tomed to the tune she
makes the day be-gin. _____ I've got-ten used to hear her say: "Good

whis-tles night and noon; Her smiles, her frowns, her ups, her downs are sec-ond
morn-ing" ev-'ry day; Her joys, her woes, her highs, her lows are sec-ond

IN WALKED BUD

By THELONIOUS MONK

THE LOOK OF LOVE
from CASINO ROYALE

Words by HAL DAVID
Music by BURT BACHARACH

Medium Rock Ballad (with much feeling)

IT NEVER ENTERED MY MIND

from HIGHER AND HIGHER

Words by LORENZ HART
Music by RICHARD RODGERS

I don't care if there's pow-der on my nose, I don't care if my hair-do is in place, I've lost the ver-y mean-ing of re-pose, I nev-er put a mud pack on my face. Oh, who'd have thought that I'd

THE LADY IS A TRAMP

from BABES IN ARMS
from WORDS AND MUSIC

Words by LORENZ HART
Music by RICHARD RODGERS

LOVE LETTERS
Theme from the Paramount Picture LOVE LETTERS

Words by EDWARD HEYMAN
Music by VICTOR YOUNG

LULLABY OF BIRDLAND

Words by GEORGE DAVID WEISS
Music by GEORGE SHEARING

MEDITATION
(Meditacáo)

Music by ANTONIO CARLOS JOBIM
Original Words by NEWTON MENDONCA
English Words by NORMAN GIMBEL

In _____ my lone - li - ness _____ When you're gone _____
Though _____ you're far a - way _____ I have on -

_____ and I'm all _____ by my - self _____ and I _____ need your _____ ca - ress. _____
- ly to close _____ my eyes _____ and you _____ are back _____ to stay. _____

_____ I _____ just think _____ of you _____
_____ I _____ just close _____ my eyes _____

MOON RIVER

from the Paramount Picture BREAKFAST AT TIFFANY'S

Words by JOHNNY MERCER
Music by HENRY MANCINI

MY FAVORITE THINGS

from THE SOUND OF MUSIC

Lyrics by OSCAR HAMMERSTEIN II
Music by RICHARD RODGERS

MY FOOLISH HEART

from MY FOOLISH HEART

Words by NED WASHINGTON
Music by VICTOR YOUNG

Slowly and expressively

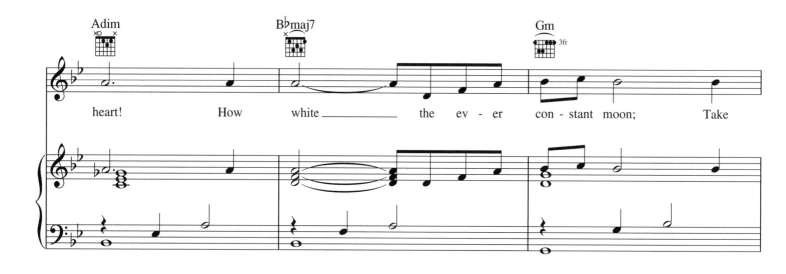

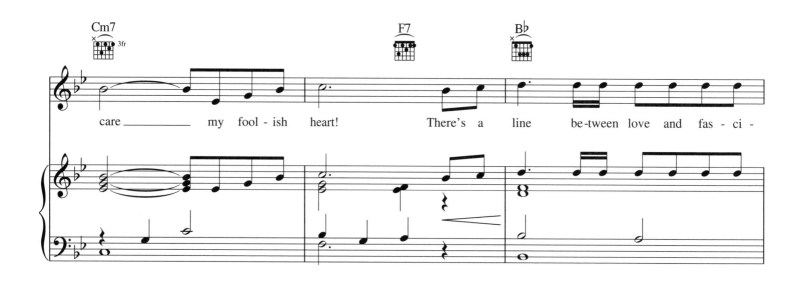

MY FUNNY VALENTINE
from BABES IN ARMS

Words by LORENZ HART
Music by RICHARD RODGERS

MY ONE AND ONLY LOVE

Words by ROBERT MELLIN
Music by GUY WOOD

A NIGHTINGALE SANG IN BERKELEY SQUARE

Lyric by ERIC MASCHWITZ
Music by MANNING SHERWIN

*Pronounced "Bar-kley"

NUAGES

By DJANGO REINHARDT
and JACQUES LARUE

Moderate Swing ♩ = 118

OH! LOOK AT ME NOW

Words by JOHN DeVRIES
Music by JOE BUSHKIN

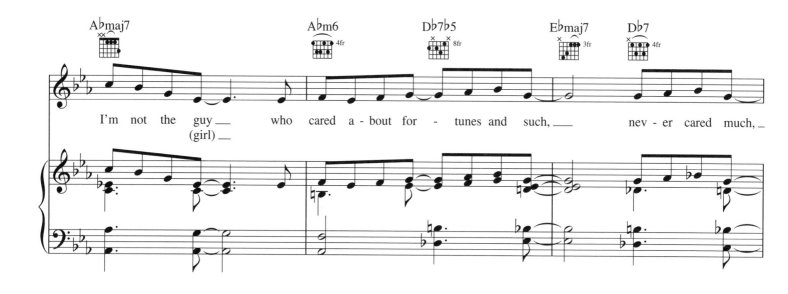

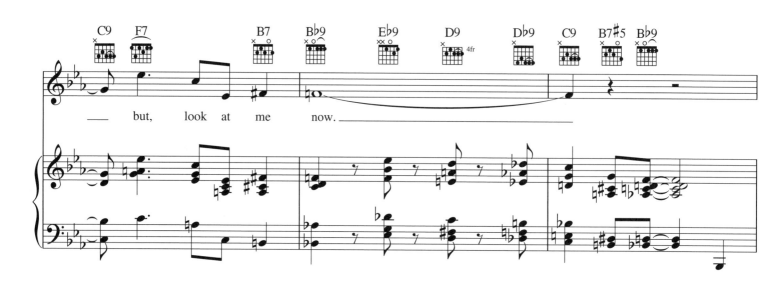

OLD DEVIL MOON

from FINIAN'S RAINBOW

Words by E.Y. HARBURG
Music by BURTON LANE

RIO DE JANEIRO BLUE

Words and Music by RICHARD TORRANCE
and JOHN HAENY

The clouds came a-creep-in' and you got me weep-in' this morn- -ing.

I can't be-lieve__ you're real- -ly gon-na leave__ this town.__

SENTIMENTAL JOURNEY

Words and Music by BUD GREEN,
LES BROWN and BEN HOMER

RUBY, MY DEAR

By THELONIOUS MONK

Speak Low
from the Musical Production ONE TOUCH OF VENUS

Words by OGDEN NASH
Music by KURT WEILL

STARDUST

Words by MITCHELL PARISH
Music by HOAGY CARMICHAEL

STOMPIN' AT THE SAVOY

Words and Music by BENNY GOODMAN,
EDGAR SAMPSON, CHICK WEBB and ANDY RAZAF

STREET LIFE

Words and Music by WILL JENNINGS
and JOE SAMPLE

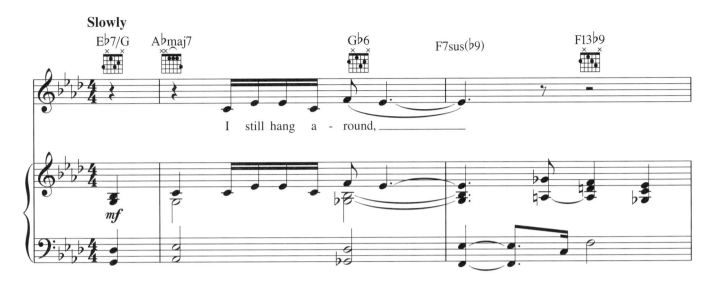

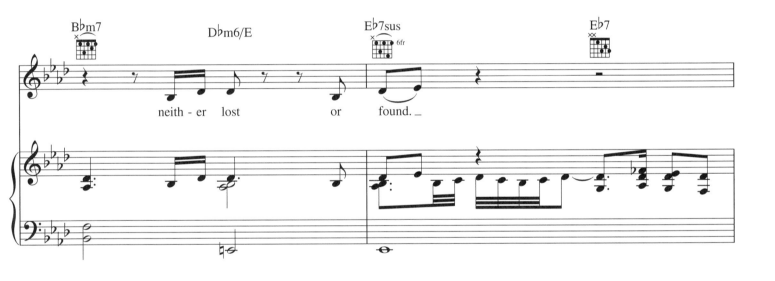

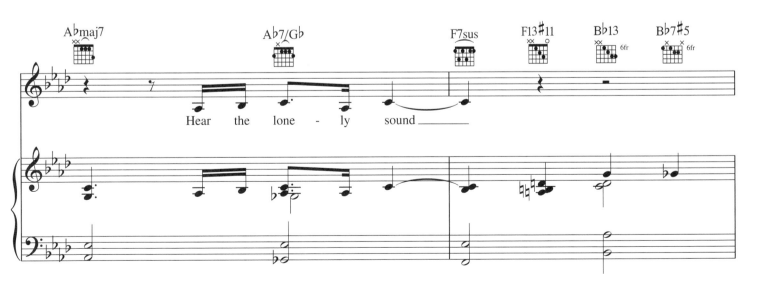

Fm7   Bbm7   Eb7sus

__ your life __ a - way. _
\- na feel __ the cold. _

You let the peo - ple see __ just
There's al - ways love _ for sale, _ a

Cm11   F7#9   Bbm7   Eb7sus

who you wan - na be, __
grown-up fair - y tale. _

and ev - 'ry night _ you shine __ just
Prince Charm - ing al - ways smiles __ be -

Abmaj7   **1** Abm7   Db7sus

like a su - per - star. __
hind a sil - ver spoon, __

That's how the life _ is played, _ a
and

Gbmaj7   Gm7b5   Bbm7   Eb7sus

ten - cent mas - quer - ade. _

You dress, you walk, _ you talk, _ you're

SUDDENLY IT'S SPRING

from the Paramount Motion Picture LADY IN THE DARK
from the Paramount Motion Picture SUDDENLY IT'S SPRING

Words by JOHNNY BURKE
Music by JAMES VAN HEUSEN

SO NICE
(Summer Samba)

Original Words and Music by MARCOS VALLE
and PAULO SERGIO VALLE
English Words by NORMAN GIMBEL

Relaxed Bossa Nova

TENDERLY
from TORCH SONG

Lyric by JACK LAWRENCE
Music by WALTER GROSS

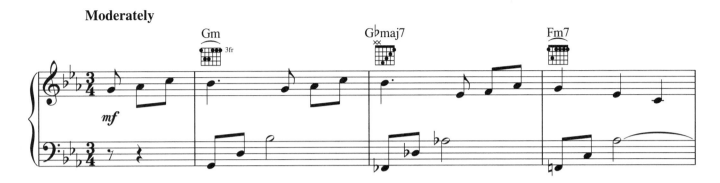

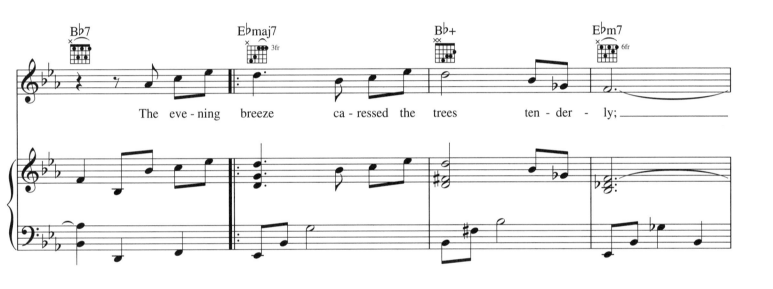

The eve-ning breeze ca-ressed the trees ten-der-ly;

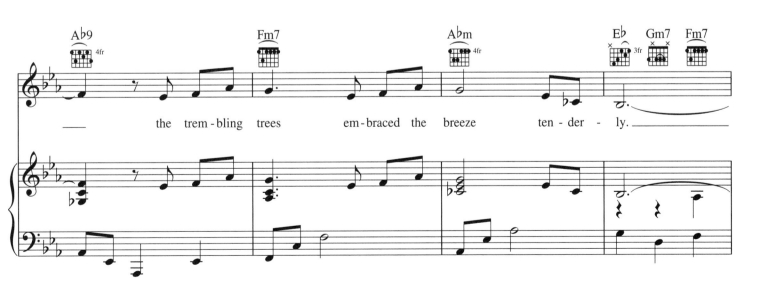

the trem-bling trees em-braced the breeze ten-der-ly.

THERE WILL NEVER BE ANOTHER YOU

from the Motion Picture ICELAND

Lyric by MACK GORDON
Music by HARRY WARREN

This is our last dance to-geth-er, _____ to-night soon will be long a - go. _____ And in our mo - ment of part - ing, _____ this is all I

THERE'S A SMALL HOTEL

from ON YOUR TOES

Words by LORENZ HART
Music by RICHARD RODGERS

WATCH WHAT HAPPENS

from THE UMBRELLAS OF CHERBOURG

Music by MICHEL LEGRAND
Original French Text by JACQUES DEMY
English Lyrics by NORMAN GIMBEL

Give that deep love to you _____ and what mag - ic you'll

see: Let some - one give his heart, Some -

1

one who cares like me. _____

2

me. _____

WHAT A DIFF'RENCE A DAY MADE

English Words by STANLEY ADAMS
Music and Spanish Words by MARIA GREVER

WHEN I FALL IN LOVE

from ONE MINUTE TO ZERO

Words by EDWARD HEYMAN
Music by VICTOR YOUNG

WHERE OR WHEN

from BABES IN ARMS

Words by LORENZ HART
Music by RICHARD RODGERS

WILLOW WEEP FOR ME

Words and Music by
ANN RONELL